01|19

D1367452

Little Inventions

THE PEN

RAPHAËL FEJTÖ

FIREFLY BOOKS

The invention of the pen is very, very ancient.
But back then, it didn't look like the pen we
know today. At the very beginning of writing,
soft clay tablets were engraved with sharp reeds.

Next, the pen was dipped in ink to write more quickly on papyrus, an early kind of paper. In Egypt, the people who wrote were called scribes. Scribes were very important: they were the ones who wrote down everything the pharaoh said.

For thousands of years, the scribes wrote about all the events of everyday life. For example, when there was a war, they took note of who won and how many people died.

One day, someone noticed that if they cut the shaft of a goose feather, and dipped that in ink, it created finer and more beautiful writing. The feathers were called quills, and in the Middle Ages,

monks used them to copy books. It was very slow work since there weren't any photocopiers or printers at the time.

Writers loved the quill and they used it to write lots of stories, poems and plays.

But the quill had a fault: it wore out quickly, and had to be sharpened or replaced often! One day, an American jeweler, Peregrine Williamson, who spent his time sharpening his boss's quills, searched for an easier way.

While visiting a friend in a steel factory, he suddenly had an idea: if his quill was made of steel, it would wear out less quickly, right?

After many attempts, he finally managed to attach a piece of wood to a metal point. Then the English improved Peregrine Williamson's quill so the ink would flow better.

A few years later, a Romanian engineer invented a pen with a reservoir of ink inside it. But it leaked a lot. It was very annoying, especially for Lewis Waterman, an American insurance agent, who spent his time signing contracts.

Lewis Waterman decided to lock himself in his workshop and perfect the invention. But the ink was either too liquid and leaked, or it was too thick and wouldn't pass through the quill...

When he found the right method,
everyone was impressed. But, at the
moment Lewis Waterman was signing
a contract, the pen leaked and made
enormous stains everywhere!

Waterman was ashamed. He swore he would find a
way to stop the pen from making stains.

After months of research, he created a pen that worked perfectly. This time, when it was time to sign his contracts, nobody made fun of him.

The pen gradually became very popular, especially among mathematicians who had to write a lot to work on their complicated equations.

At the time, a pen was a precious object,
made of rare wood that was often decorated.
It was very expensive.

So, a Hungarian journalist, Laszlo Biro tried to find a way to make a pen that was less expensive. One day, he walked past some children playing marbles next to a puddle of water.

He noticed that after the marble passed through the water, it left a very fine and precise trail of water behind it. Suddenly, he had an incredible idea. He just had to do the same thing... with a pen!

Instead of a feather, he secured a tiny ball at the end of the pen. When he wrote, the ball turned on itself and left a trail of ink on the page, just like the marble thrown by the children!

cap →

ink cartridge

microball

Laszlo Biro decided to call his invention... the ballpoint pen!

A few years later, the French baron Bich, a former director of an ink factory, thought the invention was so smart he bought Laszlo Biro's patent.

He decided to make a disposable pen: a pen so cheap that rather than having to buy ink cartridges, the pens were simply thrown in the garbage when they ran out of ink. He called them "Bic" pens.

Bic pens were very popular in many countries... but not in Japan, where people wrote with a brush. So, a Japanese company invented a new pen, with felt in the place of the ball and called it... the felt-tip pen!

The felt also allowed for the use of different colored inks. Overnight, it turned into the favorite pen of children, who used them to color in their beautiful drawings.

Today, most people use pens to write.

In factories all over the world, millions of pens are made every year!

And you,
what's your favorite
PEN
?

There you go, now you know everything
about the invention of the PEN!

But do you remember
everything you've read?

Play the MEMORY game to see
what you remember!

MEMORY GAME

1. What do you call the person who wrote down everything that happened, during the time of the pharaohs?

2. What type of bird feathers were used most often for writing?

3. What name did Baron Bich give to his disposable pen?

4. How did Laszlo Biro get the idea for his ballpoint pen?

5. What are the three of the main types of pens that exist?

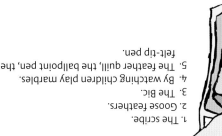

1. The scribe.
2. Goose feathers.
3. The Bic.
4. By watching children play marbles.
5. The feather quill, the ballpoint pen, the felt-tip pen.

A FIREFLY BOOK

Published by Firefly Books Ltd. 2016

Source edition © 2015 Le Stylo, ÉDITIONS PLAY BAC, 33 rue du Petit-Musc, 75004, Paris, France, 2015

This translated edition copyright © 2016 Firefly Books

First printing

Publisher Cataloging-in-Publication Data (U.S.)

Names: Fejtö, Raphaël, author. | Greenspoon, Golda, translator. | Mersereau, Claudine, translator.
Title: Pen / Raphaël Fejtö.
Description: Richmond Hill, Ontario, Canada : Firefly Books, 2016. | Series: Little Inventions | Originally published by Éditions Play Bac, Paris, 2015 as Les p'tites inventions: La Stylo | Summary: "This brief history on one of the small, overlooked inventions we use in our everyday lives, in a six-part series is geared toward children. With fun and quirky illustrations and dialog, it also comes with a memory quiz to ensure children retain what they learn" -- Provided by publisher.
Identifiers: ISBN 978-1-77085-748-3 (hardcover)
Subjects: LCSH: Pens – History -- Juvenile literature.
Classification: LCC TX1262.F458 |DDC 681.6 – dc23

Library and Archives Canada Cataloguing in Publication

Fejtö, Raphaël
[Stylo. English]
     Pen / Raphaël Fejtö.
(Little inventions)
Translation of: Le stylo.
ISBN 978-1-77085-748-3 (bound)
     1. Pens--History--Juvenile literature. I. Title. II. Title: Stylo. English.
TS1262.F4613 2016   j681'.6   C2016-900074-5

Published in the United States by
Firefly Books (U.S.) Inc.
P.O. Box 1338, Ellicott Station
Buffalo, New York 14205

Published in Canada by
Firefly Books Ltd.
50 Staples Avenue, Unit 1
Richmond Hill, Ontario L4B 0A7

Printed in China